Business Brokers and Securities Law

How to avoid becoming an unlicensed broker-dealer

PRIVATE PLACEMENT HANDBOOK SERIES: VOLUME FIVE

TITLE: BUSINESS BROKERS AND SECURITIES LAWS

SUBTITLE: How to avoid becoming an unlicensed broker-dealer

AUTHOR: Douglas Slain

PUBLISHER: Private Placement Advisors, LLC

First Edition

Published November 5, 2013

ISBN-13: 978-1493638857

ISBN-10: 1493638858

Table of Contents

Chapter One: What is the problem? 4

Chapter Two: Who is a broker-dealer? 7

Chapter Three: How can a business broker be exempt? 9

Chapter Four: What is non-compliance? 18

Chapter One: What is The Problem?

The United States Supreme Court has held that the sale of an interest in a business constitutes a securities transaction. Accordingly, the transaction is entitled to the protection of the federal securities laws. This handbook discusses broker-dealer registration requirements under The Securities Act of 1933 and the applicability of state blue sky laws to business brokers.

The recurring theme under federal and state law to determine if a business broker will be required to register as a broker-dealer or agent is whether he satisfies both the "engaged in business" and "effecting transactions" requirements. The law which has emerged in this area has resulted primarily from pronouncements by the SEC staff.

The United States Supreme Court has ruled that the definitions of a security in the Securities Act of 1933 and the Exchange Act of 1934 are virtually identical. Broker-dealers and agents may not engage in securities transactions unless they are registered with their state. Also it is unlawful for any person to transact business in their state as a broker-dealer or agent unless so licensed.

The problem is how to be compensated as a finder without violating federal and state securities laws.

Section 3(4) of the Exchange Act provides that a broker is "any person engaged in the business of effecting transactions in securities for the account of others, but does not include a bank." 15 U.S.C. § 78(a) (4) (1984). Section 15(a) (1) of the Exchange Act makes it unlawful for any broker or dealer, except for those who exclusively engage in an intrastate business, to make use of the mails or any means or instrumentality of interstate commerce to effect any transactions in, or to induce the purchase or sale of, any security (other than an exempted security or commercial paper, banker's acceptances, or commercial bills) unless such broker or dealer is registered in accordance with section 15(b).

State legislation in the area of broker-dealer regulation has also been designed to prevent unscrupulous activity and to require a minimum level of competence for those effecting security transactions. Although blue sky legislation varies from state to state, nearly all jurisdictions require the registration of broker-dealers or agents who offer securities. In addition, because most states have modeled their securities law on the 1956 Uniform Securities Act, most state securities acts apply to: evidence of indebtedness, certificates of interest or participation in any profit sharing agreement, collateral-trust certificates, preorganization certificates or subscriptions, transferable shares, investment contracts, voting-trust certificates, certificates of deposit for a security, fractional undivided interests in oil, gas, or other mineral rights, any put, call, straddle, option or privilege on any security, certificates of deposit, or group or index of securities (including any interest therein or based on the value thereof), or any put, call, straddle, option, or privilege entered into on a national securities exchange relating to foreign currency, or, in general, any interest or instrument commonly known as a "security," or any certificate of interest or participation in, temporary or interim certificate for, receipt for, guarantee of, or warrant or right to subscribe to or purchase, any of the foregoing.

Chapter Two: Who Is a Broker-Dealer?

A broker-dealer is any person engaged in the business of effecting transactions in securities for the account of others or for the person's own account. "Broker-dealer" does not include:

(a) An agent;

(b) An issuer;

(c) A bank, savings institution or trust company, when effecting transactions for its own account or as agent;

(d) An executor, administrator, guardian, conservator or pledgee; or

(e) A person licensed as a real estate broker whose transactions in securities are isolated transactions incidental to that business.

The "engaged in business" requirement implies either holding oneself out as available to perform or actually performing repeated securities transactions. Although the definition of broker does not share the "regular business" language with the definition of a dealer, it appears that more than isolated transactions are required before one must register as a securities broker.

In applying the "recurrence test," the SEC in its no-action letters has uniformly held that registration is not mandated under section 15(a) (1) of the Exchange Act if a person has never participated in securities transactions and does not anticipate making any further securities offerings." The SEC staff has stated that section 15(a) of the Exchange Act requires registration of a person who has had prior experience as a securities salesman and might become involved in future offerings.

The regularity and frequency of turnover is a decisive factor in the broker-dealer status determination. For example, a person who had repeatedly sold interests in real estate ventures to investors as part of a real estate business was held to be a "dealer" and, therefore, was required to register. Still, It is apparent that a person may be required to register as a broker-dealer although a person's securities activities neither constitute his principal business or principal source of income.

In addition, advertising by a person or entity may evidence being "engaged in business." The SEC staff has held that the utilization of advertisements to accumulate a position in a particular security will not necessarily qualify a person as a dealer if there is no repetition of the activity as to other securities. In contrast, holding oneself out as available or interested in trading through general advertising can bring one within the "engaged in business" test.

Chapter Three: How Can a Business Broker be Exempt?

There are three types of exemptions for business brokers from registration as a broker or dealer:

(A) those arising from the market in which transactions occur;

(B) those arising from the kinds of securities involved; and

(C) those arising from the type of individual involved in the distribution of the securities.

Section 15(a) of the Exchange Act provides that a broker-dealer "whose business is exclusively intrastate and who does not make use of any facility of a national securities exchange" is exempted from the registration requirement. The word "exclusively" is strictly construed. A few transactions over the course of many years or even a single transaction which crosses state lines may destroy the exemption. The intrastate business will integrate with the interstate transactions thus destroying the exemption.

The SEC has integrated the activities of an individual selling on an intrastate basis with the activities of another individual selling in different states for the same issuer so as to deny the exemption. The SEC staff has also refused to sanction an exemption for any officer, director, or employee of the issuer who will engage in an offering and will be paid a commission as a broker if any such individual "has previously engaged in a securities business in a state other than the state in which the issuer proposes to offer its securities." The SEC has also held that both the broker's and issuer's businesses must be in the same state. For example, a broker-dealer would be required to register if he participated in a single offering of securities of an out-of-state issuer notwithstanding the following: (1) the broker-dealer's business was exclusively intrastate; (2) sales would be made only to residents of the broker's state; and (3) trading of the securities would be limited to the broker's state.

Section 15(a) of the Exchange Act states that it is unlawful for an unregistered broker-dealer to effect any transaction or induce the purchase or sale of any security other than an exempted security or commercial paper. Consequently, if a broker-dealer effects any transaction in nonexempt securities he must register even though he may be dealing primarily in exempted securities.

Pursuant to section 15(a) (2) of the Exchange Act, the SEC adopted Rule 3a4-1 which defines the "safe harbor" circumstances under which persons associated? with an issuer, such as officers, directors or employees, who participate in a distribution of the issuer's securities, shall be deemed not to be brokers subject to registration.

"Exempted security" as referred to in section 15(a) of the Exchange Act is defined in section (3) (a) (12) of the Act to include, as of July 25, 1987, the following:

(I) government securities, as defined in paragraph (42) of this subsection;

(ii) Municipal securities, as defined in paragraph (29) of this subsection;

(iii) Any interest or participation in any common trust fund or similar fund maintained by a bank exclusively for the collective investment and reinvestment of assets contributed thereto by such bank in its capacity as trustee, executor, administrator, or guardian;

(iv) any interest or participation in a single trust fund, or a collective trust fund maintained by a bank, or any security arising out of a contract issued by an insurance company, which interest, participation, or security is issued in connection with a qualified plan as defined in subparagraph (C) of this paragraph; and

(v) such other securities (which may include, among others, unregistered securities, the market in which is predominantly intrastate) as the Commission may, by such rules and regulations as it deems consistent with the public interest and the protection of investors, either unconditionally or upon specified terms and conditions or for stated periods, exempt from the operation of any one or more provisions of this chapter which by their terms do not apply to an "exempted security" or to "exempted securities."

Assuming satisfaction of the above requirements, the safe harbor may be utilized by an "associated person" may qualify under the safe harbor rule if the person performs substantial duties on behalf of an issuer in connection with transactions in securities, provided that the person was neither a broker-dealer nor an associated person of a broker-dealer within the preceding twelve months and the person does "not participate in selling an offering of securities for any issuer more than once every 12 months."

The "engaged in business" requirement implies either holding oneself out as available to perform or actually performing repeated securities transactions. Although the definition of broker does not share the "regular business" language with the definition of a dealer, it appears that more than isolated transactions are required before one must register as a securities broker.

In applying the "recurrence test," the SEC in its no-action letters has uniformly held that registration is not mandated under section 15(a) (1) of the Exchange Act if a person has never participated in securities transactions and does not anticipate making any further securities offerings." The SEC staff has stated that section 15(a) of the Exchange Act requires registration of a person who has had prior experience as a securities salesman and might become involved in future offerings.

The regularity and frequency of turnover is a decisive factor in the broker-dealer status determination. For example, a person who had repeatedly sold interests in real estate ventures to investors as part of a real estate business was held to be a "dealer" and, therefore, was required to register. Still, It is apparent that a person may be required to register as a broker-dealer although a person's securities activities neither constitute his principal business or principal source of income.

In addition, advertising by a person or entity may evidence being "engaged in business." The SEC staff has held that the utilization of advertisements to accumulate a position in a particular security will not necessarily qualify a person as a dealer if there is no repetition of the activity as to other securities. In contrast, holding oneself out as available or interested in trading through general advertising can bring one within the "engaged in business" test.

Typically, there are five activities related to the functions of a registered securities broker-dealer or agent which may bring one within the definition of a broker-dealer or agent: (1) acting as a finder; (2) consulting independently with an issuer; (3) channeling customers to broker-dealers; (4) sharing in broker-dealer compensation; or (5) maintaining custody or possession of customers' funds or securities.

Generally, a finder brings together two entities interested in forming a business.

The services of finders may vary from case to case. If a finder merely brings the parties together with no involvement in negotiating the price or any of the other terms of the transaction, he will not be acting as a broker.

On the other hand, a finder will be deemed to be a broker if he participates in negotiations by advising on questions of value or performs other acts to facilitate the transaction. The SEC staff has taken the position those individuals who do nothing more than bring merger or acquisition-minded persons or entities together and do not participate in negotiations or settlements probably are not brokers or dealers. On the other hand, persons who play an integral role in negotiating and effecting mergers or acquisitions that involve transactions in securities generally are deemed to be either a broker or dealer.

The SEC staff has addressed whether a business broker was required to register as a broker under section 15(a) of the Exchange Act. The staff did not recommend enforcement action against the business broker even though the broker entered into listing agreements with businesses to sell the assets of these companies, advertised the assets of these companies, provided information supplied by the seller to prospective buyers, assisted in negotiations by transmitting documents between parties, and collected a commission based on the selling price. In taking this position the staff noted that a business broker need not register because: (1) he had a limited role in negotiations between the seller and buyer; (2) the businesses involved were going concerns; (3) only assets were advertised; (4) transactions effected by sales of securities would involve the sale of all the equity to one buyer or a group formed without the business broker's assistance; (5) no advice was rendered by the business broker as to whether to issue securities nor did it assess the value of securities sold; (6) the compensation did not vary according to whether the form of the transaction was an asset or stock sale; and (7) the business broker did not assist the buyers in obtaining financing, except that it could, at the parties' request, provide a list of potential lenders.

To avoid broker-dealer status, a business broker must not assist or supervise the sales efforts of a securities offering. The business broker must limit his activities to advising the issuer on how to develop the offering. In *Church Of Christ v. National Plan, Inc.*, the court of appeals held that the evidence conclusively established that the business broker was a securities broker where the he: (1) assisted the issuer in doing all of the legal work concerning the offering; (2) completed all necessary printing; (3) handled all of the paper work in connection with the offering; (4) served as fiscal agent and trustee of the offering; (5) put on programs relating to the offering. The SEC staff held that a consultant retained to develop a proposed business plan of a new corporation, including the program for offering securities, need not register as a broker-dealer.

However the SEC staff concluded that registration would be required where a firm engaged in the following activities: (1) conducted a feasibility study to structure the issuance of securities; (2) prepared an outline for the issuer with recommendations relating to the issue; (3) searched out and obtained a registered broker-dealer to act as managing underwriter; (4) prepared the registration statement and handled it's processing; (5) assisted broker-dealers and their representatives in analyzing and developing marketing techniques with respect to the offering; (6) provided training programs for representatives of the broker-dealers upon request; and (7) received a commission based on the size of the offering.

In determining whether a person is a broker-dealer, the SEC staff has also examined whether the compensation is fixed as opposed to being transaction-based. The SEC has concluded that attorneys, accountants, insurance brokers, and financial service organizations "who for a fee assist promoters or other issuers in the sale of securities" is considered to be brokers if they have been "retained by an issuer specifically for the purpose of selling securities to the public and generally receive transaction-based compensation." However, the SEC staff held that registration was not required where someone received negotiated fees relating to "the overall size of the financing that the client wished to arrange, which generally would not be payable unless the financing ends successfully."

In a 1974 no-action letter, the SEC took a no-action position on a finder whose activities included introducing parties to negotiate acquisitions of businesses or assets. The finder did not become involved in the negotiations of parties or evaluation of the proposed transaction. However, the SEC indicated that if the finder's business included solicitation of investors' indications of interest in a security, the finder would be deemed an underwriter as defined in section 2(11) of the Securities Act.

Chapter Four: What is Non-Compliance?

The sale of a security by an unregistered broker-dealer or agent may result in both civil and criminal liability for the broker-dealer or agent and the issuer or seller.

The civil remedies available to a purchaser of securities from an unlicensed broker-dealer may be classified into three categories: remedies at common law; express or implied remedies under federal law; and express or implied remedies under state blue sky laws. In addition to the civil remedies, the Securities and Exchange Commission as well as the Commissioner of Securities for the relevant state is empowered to obtain injunctions against unregistered persons engaging in securities brokerage activity.

The courts are divided about whether there is an implied right of recovery under the Exchange Act for buyers or sellers of securities when a broker or dealer fails to register under section 15(a) of the Act. Section 15(a), by its terms, does not mandate express liability for its violation. Hence, courts have generally held that there is no private right of action for violations of section 15 of the Exchange Act. But if state securities commissioner's office has reason to believe that any security is being or has been offered or sold in his state by any unlicensed person, the commissioner may by order summarily prohibit such person from further offers or sales of securities in this state until licensed.

Also, courts have held that a private cause of action can be founded upon section 29(b) of the Act. Section 29(b) provides: [e]very contract made in violation of any provision of [the Act] ... and every contract ... the performance of which involves the violation of ... any provision of [the Act] ...shall be void ... as regards the rights of any person who, in violation of any such provision ... shall have made or engaged in the performance of any such contract."

Section 29(b) of the Exchange Act permits a party to a contract to seek rescission if he can show that "(1) the contract involved a 'prohibited transaction' [under the Exchange Act], (2) he is in contractual privity with the defendant and (3) he is 'in the class of persons the Act was designed to protect. Notwithstanding the courts' refusal to imply a private cause of action under section 15(a), courts have held that section 29(b) creates an implied private cause of action for rescission or similar equitable relief. Consequently, a section 29(b) claim can be based on an Exchange Act provision that does not contain private rights of action but the ordinary equitable defenses of estoppel, waiver and laches are applicable.

In determining whether injunctive relief is warranted under the federal securities laws, courts have examined whether "there is a reasonable likelihood of further violation in the future. "Addressing this issue in the context of a broker-dealer's failure to register, a district court examined the following factors: (1) the likelihood of future violations; (2) the degree of scanter involved; (3) the sincerity of defendant's assurances against future violations; (4) the isolated or recurrent nature of the infraction; (5) defendant's recognition of the wrongful nature of his conduct; and (6) the likelihood, because of defendant's professional occupation, that those future violations might occur. Given the unregistered broker's history of securities law violations, the court granted a permanent injunction. Although the degree of scanter may be a factor as to whether an injunction should be issued, it has been held in a case involving a claim for injunctive relief, that section 15(a) (1) contains no language from which a scanter requirement may be derived.

Courts have also enjoined a person from advertising when such conduct would cause the person to qualify as a broker-dealer. For example, a person who advertised in a newspaper with interstate circulation that he could save customers seventy percent on their brokerage commissions and that no commissions would be charged if the customer maintained a $500 balance in his account was enjoined for not registering as a broker-dealer.

Section 15(b) (4) of the Exchange Act sets forth the Commission's authority to institute disciplinary proceedings against broker-dealers. Under this section the

Commission may order any of the following for a willful failure to register:

(1) censure;
(2) limitations on activities, functions or operations;
(3) suspension of registration for a period not to exceed twelve months; and,
(4) revocation of registration.

In addition, the Commission may order any of the above if one is permanently or temporarily enjoined from acting as a broker-dealer.

The Commission also has the authority to suspend the registration of a broker-dealer pending a final determination of whether the registration should be revoked. As previously noted, a purchaser of securities may seek rescission under section 29(b) of the Exchange Act. Thus, a rescission action under section 29(b) based upon a section 15 (a) violation will have a greater impact on a seller or an issuer than the broker-dealer if it results in the business sale being voided.

Although a purchaser of securities can obtain equitable relief against an issuer or seller, it is doubtful that money damages can be obtained. Moreover, given the absence of an implied right of action under section 15 (a), it is unlikely that a purchaser of securities could rely on section 20(a) of the Exchange Act to impose liability on a seller of a business. Section 20(a) provides that a controlling person may be jointly and severally liable with the controlled person for securities violations under certain circumstances.

However, the common law action of respondent superior may be available to a purchaser of securities against a seller or issuer if an unlicensed broker-dealer was engaged to sell a business. Thus, a rescission action under section 29(b) based upon a section 15(a) violation will have a greater impact on a seller or an issuer than the broker-dealer if it results in the business sale being voided. Although a purchaser of securities can obtain equitable relief against an issuer or seller, it is doubtful that money damages can be obtained.

Moreover, given the absence of an implied right of action under section 15(a), it is unlikely that a purchaser of securities could rely on section 20(a) of the Exchange Act to impose liability on a seller of a business. Section 20(a) provides that a controlling person may be jointly and severally liable with the controlled person for securities violations under certain circumstances. However, the common law action of respondent superior may be available to a purchaser of securities against a seller or issuer if an unlicensed broker-dealer was engaged to sell a business. Finally, although no implied cause of action under section 15(a) exists; the Commission is not precluded from enjoining the issuer or bringing Criminal sanctions against the issuer for employing an unregistered broker-dealer.

A court may impose criminal sanctions for all of the violations previously discussed with respect to civil liabilities. These violations include: (1) section

551.21(1), offering un-registered nonexempt securities; (2) section 551.31(1), unlicensed broker-dealer or agent; (3) section 551.31(2), broker-dealer or issuer employing unlicensed agent; (4) section 551.31(2), agent representing more than one broker-dealer or issuer at any one time; and (5) section 551.31(6), licensed broker-dealer or agent transacting business in violation of Chapter 551.

Judge Reynolds of the Eastern District Federal Court stated that "[I]t is the nature of the act which is dispositive, not the state of mind of the actor." In this sense, the statute imposes a form of strict liability. Once the seller has "willfully engaged in conduct which operates or would operate as a fraud or deceit ... he will not be heard to argue that he did not intend the consequences of his acts" or unethical practices in the security business.

Business brokers and agents should consider the following courses of action: First, you need to minimize the scope of activities in connection with the sale of a business. This may be accomplished by merely introducing the parties and not engaging in substantive business negotiations on behalf of the parties. Alternatively, if the business broker effects a controlling interest stock sale which, but for the payment of commission, would have been eligible for a '; stock transactional exemption pursuant to sections 551.23(10), (11) or (19), or would have been otherwise exempt under section 551.23(1), then a request should be made upon the state Commissioner of Securities for an order finding that registration of the stock sale and the business broker is not necessary or appropriate for the protection of investors.

If the business broker has passed the required exams, he may be licensed in the state as an agent of the issuer and receive commissions without jeopardizing the applicable transactional exemption, but the securities transaction should be exclusively intrastate; otherwise, federal broker-dealer licensing may be required, allowing a purchaser to seek civil remedies against the broker and seller under federal law.

As always, a no-action request to the SEC as to whether the business broker would be deemed a broker-dealer under the factual circumstances could be appropriate if there is sufficient time to await a response. Although this approach provides some level of comfort, the SEC's position will not be binding upon purchasers of stock in the event the business fail and the purchaser seeks private civil remedies.

The legislative history of the Exchange Act and state blue sky laws indicate an intent to regulate the competence and character of those effecting securities transactions. The applicant initiates the process by filing a Form BD together with accompanying exhibits with the SEC. Special forms are required for areas of practice, including municipal securities. Once an application is accepted for filing, the SEC, within 45 days, will grant registration or institute proceedings to determine whether registration should be denied. A broker-dealer must not commence doing business until its registration has been granted and its officers, directors and other employees have satisfied certain requirements.

About the author

Douglas Slain received a JD from Stanford Law School, a MA from the University of Chicago, and a BA from DePauw University. After practicing real estate and business law at Pillsbury, Madison & Sutro, he founded four national monthly law reporting titles now owned by Thomson-Reuters. He was also chairman of the American Bar Association's General Practice section's Professional Responsibility Committee.

Slain was an ABA-appointed rule of law consultant to the Ministry of Economy for the Republic of Latvia as its secured transactions adviser. He taught for one semester at Stanford Law School as an adjunct clinical law professor.
Slain is the managing partner of Private Placement Advisors, LLC; the founder of RegDConsumersReport.com; and the owner/manager of a LinkedIn discussion group with over 1,300 members.

www.ingramcontent.com/pod-product-compliance
Lightning Source LLC
Chambersburg PA
CBHW070736180526
45167CB00004B/1776